EGYPTIAN TOMB

Conceived and created
by Claude Delafosse
and Gallimard Jeunesse
Illustrated by
Sabine Krawczyk

HIDDEN WORLD

A FIRST DISCOVERY BOOK

SCHOLASTIC INC.
New York   Toronto   London   Auckland   Sydney
Mexico City   New Delhi   Hong Kong

Join the archaeologists
while they investigate
a newly opened tomb.
What treasures
you will find there!

This book will
show you the
incredible art
of the ancient
Egyptians.

As you explore its pages with
a simple paper flashlight,
you will discover the
world inside an
Egyptian tomb.

To start exploring the tomb, remove the paper
flashlight from the back of the book.

In the next room, the walls
are covered with carvings.
One scene shows
Nenufar eating a meal.

Egyptians believed
that the dead
would need food
in the afterlife, so
they placed dishes
and drinking cups
inside the tomb.

Move the flashlight
between the black pages and the plastic pages
to uncover hidden images.

Over 4,500 years ago, the ancient Egyptians
built huge pyramids that contained
elaborate burial chambers for royalty.

Ordinary men and women were buried
in tombs cut into the sides of cliffs.
Archaeologists study these tombs
to learn about the Egyptians.

This extraordinary civilization still has
many secrets to share.

Look! A tunnel has been found. From the markings on the wall, it is clear that it will lead to a tomb. These markings are pictures that represent the name of the person buried here. The picture writing of the ancient Egyptians is called hieroglyphs.

This little person tells us that the pictures spell a woman's name.

The name of the woman buried here is Nenufar.

The page on the right shows which picture stands for which letter or sound. Use your flashlight to spell out Nenufar.

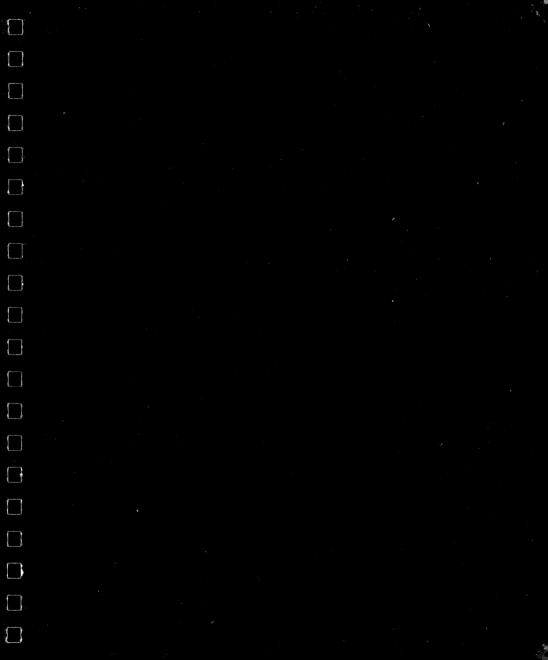

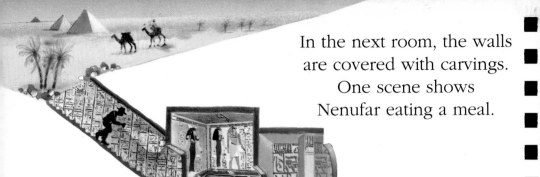

In the next room, the walls are covered with carvings. One scene shows Nenufar eating a meal.

Egyptians believed that the dead would need food in the afterlife, so they placed dishes and drinking cups inside the tomb.

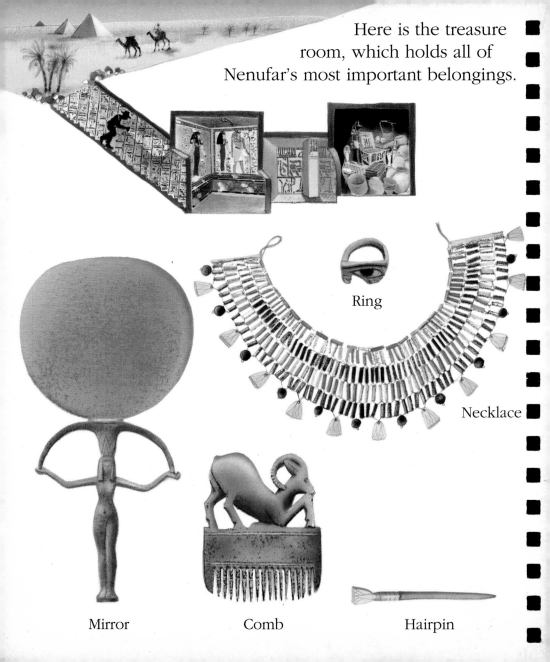

Here is the treasure room, which holds all of Nenufar's most important belongings.

Ring

Necklace

Mirror

Comb

Hairpin

The last room is
the burial chamber itself.

It contains a sarcophagus, a decorated
stone coffin. The coffin is surrounded
by paintings of ancient Egyptian gods.

| Anubis | Thoth | Isis | Horus | Osiris |

Egyptian gods

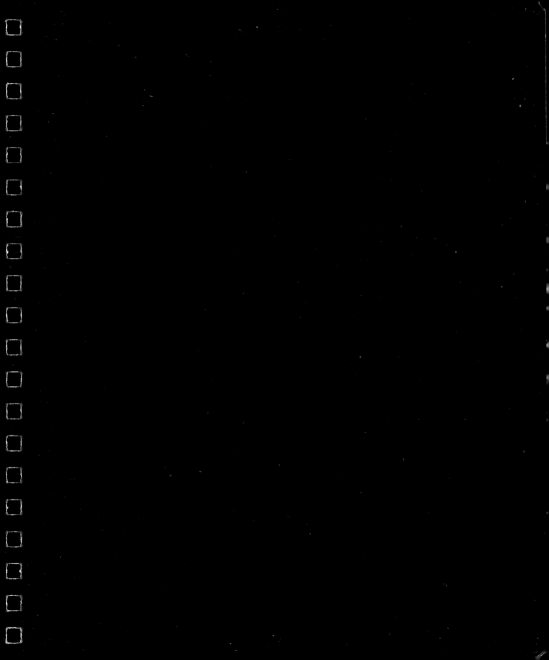

To preserve the body, Egyptians used
a process called embalming.

The body was flushed out with water and purified.

The inner organs were removed and placed in special jars.

Then the body was stuffed with straw or wood chips

and wrapped in strips of cloth, creating a mummy.

Pieces of this fascinating world of
ancient Egypt can be found in museums
around the country and the world.

There you can get close
to these marvelous objects
and learn more about
this awesome and
important culture.

Did you find these hidden images . . .

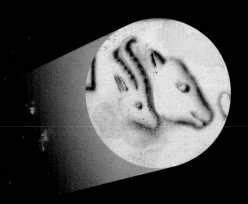

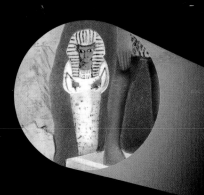

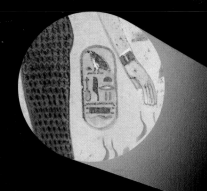

...with your magic paper flashlight?

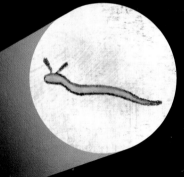

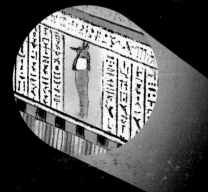

Library of Congress Cataloging-in-Publication Data available.

Originally published in France in 1998 under the title *le tombeau égyptien* by Editions Gallimard Jeunesse.

ISBN 0-439-06776-6

10 9 8 7 6 5 4 3 2 1   9/9 0/0 01 02 03

Printed in Italy by Editoriale Lloyd
First Scholastic printing, August 1999